Pints c

Encounters Down the Pub

Peter Howell-Jones
Canon Missioner at Birmingham Cathedral
and Bishop's Adviser for Mission

Nick Wills
Priest-in-Charge of St Andrew's, Kettering

GROVE BOOKS LIMITED
RIDLEY HALL RD CAMBRIDGE CB3 9HU

Contents

Church Army supports the Grove Evangelism Series

Church Army is a society of evangelists within the Anglican Communion that trains, supports and deploys evangelists across the UK and Ireland to enable people to come to a living faith in Jesus Christ.

Church Army — sharing faith through words and action

For more information about Church Army go to www.churcharmy.org.uk or phone 0208 309 3519 or email info@churcharmy.org.uk

Church Army, Marlowe House, 109 Station Rd, Sidcup, Kent DA15 7AD
Registered Charity number: 226226

First Impression November 2005
ISSN 1367-0840
ISBN 1 85174 606 4

'In the Beginning'

1

- Do you want to help people meet Jesus?
- Do you want to raise your church's profile in your local area?
- Do you want actively to engage with people where they are?
- Do you want to stir up your church?

At the turn of the millennium we said 'yes' to these questions, and began to ask another: 'How?' This booklet is the story of the journey that followed, and the profound missiological challenges it threw up. We hope that as you read it you will not only see that your church *can* go on a similar journey, but that you will actually *want to*.

'What sort of church events would you feel comfortable to invite your friends to?' An older and long established member of the congregation responded, 'I wouldn't invite them to a church event they wouldn't come!' When pushed, 'Bill' was happy to talk about his faith in Jesus, but reluctant to invite his friends along to church. The cultural gap between the world his friends inhabited and the church he attended was, as he put it, 'too great.' When challenged: 'If we were to run an event in a local pub would you bring your friends?' 'Bill' promised he would and *Pints of View* was born.

The cultural gap between the world his friends inhabited and the church he attended was, as he put it, 'too great'

Initial Endeavours—A One-off Event

The millennium, we were told, was going to be a significant opportunity to get people thinking about Jesus. But in the light of conversations with 'Bill,' we became increasingly aware of the dangers of merely 'adopting' one of the many creative marketing strategies for engaging people outside the church in the hope that they would 'come in and find faith.' We raised the idea of a pub event with a small group of people within the church and their response was favourable. So work began turning the idea into a reality.

We were conscious of the fact that working in a pub or similar non-church environment was nothing new for Christians. Enquirers' courses and guest events are increasingly common. However, none of our team thinking through the idea had any personal experience of working in a pub—although one member had worked behind a bar for a couple of years during student days! Questions were raised with regard to format, length, location, content and importantly duration. We were convinced right from the start that the ethos of the event was crucial. People had to feel comfortable, secure and on a level playing field. This might be a church-initiated event but our aim was to listen and respond to the questions that people had rather than start from the perspective of us telling them what we thought they needed to know. The outcome of our conversations resulted in a series of three Question and Answer sessions on consecutive Monday evenings during January 2000. A recently opened pub on the high street provided an ideal venue after agreement with the management. All that was left for us to do was to decide the format and produce publicity.

Our aim was to listen and respond rather than start from the perspective of us telling them what we thought they needed to know

Recognizing our desire to listen and respond, we considered a simple question and answer format the most appropriate way to begin. We limited ourselves to a 90-minute session starting at 8pm with opportunity for informal table conversation after the formal close at 9.30pm. For each of the three weeks neither of us left the pub before closing and on two occasions conversations carried on as we walked home.

Early Reflections

Throughout, we had a good response from church and non-church people alike. During February 2000 we began to reflect on how the event had been received and how we considered it had gone. The landlord of the pub was positive. This probably had more to do with his increased sales on a Monday night than anything else! From the panellists' perspective, the three-week experience was considerably easier than first expected. Our initial apprehension soon gave way to a genuine sense of excitement and fulfilment for a good night's work. Clearly, there were issues to address, but for a first stab at pub ministry we were pleased.

Members of our congregation were equally surprised at how straightforward and uncomplicated the whole event was. They were comfortable to invite friends and happy themselves to ask questions that they had never had the confidence to ask in a church environment.

Punters in the pub who had not been invited to the event not only listened in but on occasions actively participated. What is more, there was no sense of 'us invading their space' but rather a real acceptance of us being there. As a group we considered that it 'felt' good as a point of connecting with others.

Our decision to have two panellists proved to be a good one on two levels. First, it provided good moral support when your mind went blank and words refused to come—it does happen even to 'professionals.' But secondly, and more importantly, two people provide variety of voice and viewpoint. For many sitting in the pub it was encouraging to see two people sharing the same platform and at times seeing things from a completely different perspective and still going away as friends.

From the perspective of response we were delighted to see two men start to attend our church. 'Brian' had been a member of a local church, but following a bereavement, had found it harder to belong to that community and drifted out of church life. He saw an article in the local press about the *Pints of View* event at Boldmere and came along. He kept coming for several months, got to know us, then came along to a church service and eventually became a committed member of our church.

'Dave' had recently moved into the area and wanted to find out a little more about Christianity. His wife had attended the church, heard about *Pints of View* and sent him along. The open environment paved the way for him to join an *Emmaus* course and later make a commitment to following Jesus.

Holding this event in a well-used local pub certainly raised the profile of the church in the local community. In the weeks that followed we had conversations with a number of non-church goers who had been in the pub on one of the three nights we had been there. We also found that 'regulars' to the pub would speak to us when we called in for a drink ourselves.

> *Holding this event in a well-used local pub certainly raised the profile of the church*

It was clear that all those who had been involved with this experiment were glad they had done it and wanted to explore the possibility of continuing. The church was certainly helped to feel good about itself—it was 'doing evangelism.'

Stage Two—Developing a Monthly Event

As the excitement began to die down numerous people started to ask when we would be running the next event. Good question. Our original intention was to stage a one-off event but, clearly, there was scope for more. We began the process of thinking through what a more regular event might look like.

Three consecutive weeks had taken its toll. We were tired, and honest enough to recognize that continuing at this level would simply not be sustainable. The general consensus was to continue, but only on the first Monday of each month.

Now that the wider church had begun to understand the principles behind the pub initiative it was not too long before it became a recognized mission engagement strategy for the church, a sort of bridge-building event accessible to all. Friends who were visiting church members on a Monday would regularly be brought along, together with work colleagues, family members and neighbours. The format seemed to work well but there were still areas in need of development.

We had to develop a campaign logo that would be professional enough to stand alongside other in-house material

By working outside the church environment we were constantly reminded of the need for professionalism and quality. Menu cards, posters behind the bar, the in-house magazine on the table, were all produced to the highest standard. Our first attempt at publicity for the three-week campaign had been produced on a limited budget and printed on a photocopier. Now that we were here to stay we decided that we had to improve our image and develop a campaign logo that would be distinctive and professional enough to stand alongside other in-house material.

Nick has a natural ability not only with words but with design as well. Our first full year's campaign was launched with publicity in the form of a bookmark with the title 'Use your Head.'

USE YOUR HEAD
listen, think, chat and drink

It was well-received and Peter became a well known face as a consequence. Towards the end of the first year, we decided to prepare new publicity with a new campaign logo. *Pints of View* was that year's favourite, and suitable glossy publicity was produced (see front cover). Year three saw the launch of 'Answers on Tap' and year four tried to make links with a logo already recognized within any real ale pub—'Campaign for Real Questions.'

Campaign For Real Questions

Year on year our relationships with the pub and people in the area grew. A journalist from the local paper frequently rang to see how things were going and would run an article at least twice a year. Newspaper coverage led to the local Radio Station contacting Peter for a number of interviews. *Pints of View* was beginning to establish itself in the life of the local community and for the church there was a positive feel with regard to engaging outside the church walls.

Stage Three—Local Celebrities

By the end of the first full year we had grown in confidence and understanding of how best to engage in the pub environment. It became increasingly apparent that many questions would reappear in different guises and it was important to recognize this particularly if your answers might have changed—regulars had particularly good memories.

As much as we enjoyed presenting and wrestling with the questions raised we decided that further development in this area would be valuable. We then began to explore the possibility of asking three or four people with specific areas of speciality to come and participate in a similar way. Over the next two years we were pleased to welcome four bishops, an oncologist, a high court judge and a toxicologist, all of whom were able to engage their understanding of faith in effective and engaging ways.

One further developmer was a growing willingness from people within the 'audience' to participate themselves

One further development was a growing willingness from people within the 'audience' to participate themselves. This grew over time and was certainly helped by inviting guest panellists. To see people begin to articulate their own thoughts and reflect theologically in a pub environment was certainly not something we would have envisaged two years before.

The process of establishing *Pints of View* as a fixed part of the church's life and witness in the community was an emerging one. We had certainly not worked everything out from the start and as time went by we found ourselves responding to events, suggestions and ideas that arose. Flexibility and openness to change were, on reflection, crucial to the growing success of this emerging event.

Flexibility and openness to change were crucial to the growing success of this emerging event

At the time of writing we have helped establish two other events in different parts of the country.

In Catshill, in Worcestershire, the Vicar, Craig Smith, began a *Pints of View* event in 2003. Hosted in a room off a carvery restaurant, the format differs slightly in that a guest panellist is invited every month. This has given Craig more opportunities to sit alongside people and develop relationships, rather than relating in a primarily presentational style.

Nick moved from Boldmere to become Priest-in-Charge of an urban parish in Kettering, Northants. He spent a while finding the right pub, and eventually persuaded a town centre pub to let him have a room free each month. It follows a similar format to the original *Pints of View* events, but with a guest speaker alongside Nick answering the questions.

These events both reflect the resources available in the local area and church. As with any church initiative, the crucial thing is authenticity. Simply adopting other people's ideas without going through the difficult process of examining your own context and church situation will inevitably bring its own set of problems.

As with any church initiative, the crucial thing is authenticity

2

Picture the Scene?

Monday 3rd January 2000, 7.30pm. The Vicar is in the upstairs seating area of the Bishop Vesey Pub, Boldmere. The Curate is on his way there, walking from his house nearby. The pub is not busy, but there are a few people in downstairs already, and it will fill up in the next few hours. The Vicar sits at a table, nursing a pint. The curate joins him and questions flood through their minds. Not the questions that will be fired at them later that evening — different questions; anxious questions. Questions which belie the confidence and front required to pull this thing off. Questions like:

- Is anyone going to turn up?
- Who will turn up? Will people get drunk and aggressive?
- Will anyone ask decent questions?
- Will I be able to answer the questions?
- Will I ramble on?
- Will I make a fool of myself?
- Will I be assaulted?

I guess they are the kind of questions you may be asking yourself if you consider doing something like this. Questions that now, with the benefit of hindsight and experience we can give some pretty re-assuring answers to (No one has thumped us *yet*...). The day you are not nervous is when you should really worry.

The Venue

From the outset our primary concern was to ensure that the event was as easy for people to come to as possible. The choice of venue was therefore important. It needed to be somewhere people were happy to go to themselves and invite their friends to. Somewhere that felt normal, a natural place for them to be. The atmosphere of the pub and its location was very important.

The pub where we held the events in Boldmere, The Bishop Vesey, was perfect in many ways. The owners, the J D Wetherspoon's chain, have a no music policy which meant, except on the busiest nights, that audibility was better than might be expected. It is in the middle of the High Street, and so is well known, central to the community for those who walked, with reasonable parking for those who drove, and also close to public transport links.

The pub has an upstairs gallery area which the manager was willing to allow us to use. This meant that an area could be reserved relatively straightforwardly, and we did not get in the face of those who did not want to join us.

Profile in the Community

Many people still identify church primarily with a building, and a church's membership as those who shut themselves inside that building. The *Pints of View* event gave us the opportunity to bust that myth. We were repositioned to the heart of the community, in the High Street, where in particular young and middle aged men could be seen in higher numbers than in most churches. We were visible; even the people in the pub who did not come and sit with us still noticed us.

Building Relationships

Building relationships requires two things: time and honesty. The *Pints of View* event offered us opportunities to really get to know people, as we spent time together, as they told us which issues mattered to them, and as we tried to be open and honest in wrestling with those issues. Some members of the church who would not naturally have pushed themselves forward into leadership or committee roles had a place in which to be heard and to talk. It also meant that we had something slightly different to which to invite newcomers to the church, so that they could get to know a few other members of the church in a more social environment.

Often, evangelistic events are wrapped up in an attractive outer layer, in order to make them appealing: a nice dinner party with a 'short talk' at the end, for example. When we are up front about the fact that this will happen, there is not a problem. When it is half-disclosed in an embarrassed fashion, or rushed through apologetically, there is a real possibility that relationships with seekers will be damaged rather than built-up. The *Pints of View* event is completely up front and honest; it does what it says on the postcard. Those who come are those who genuinely have questions to ask, and in taking their questions seriously, relationships with them can be strengthened. John's gospel tells us that Nicodemus came to Jesus at night to ask him some questions. Now, we cannot prove this was at a pub event, but the principle is the same.

From time to time, when we have gone in to do the event we have met people in the pub with whom we have had contact through baptisms, marriages and funerals. Some have joined us, others just had a quick chat, whilst still others have deliberately come to the event to meet up with us.

3

Why Did We Do It?
—A Theology of Engagement

Down to Earth Mission—Incarnation and the Church

Jesus gave his disciples a rough and ready, simple-to-understand model for mission and ministry:

> 'Get out there and get on with it. If they welcome you, great, if they don't, go somewhere else until you find someone who will.'
> (Luke 9.1–6)

Christians put off doing evangelism and mission. In the end there is no substitute for getting out there and getting on with it. That was Jesus' incarnational model of ministry—going out and seeing what happened, throwing the word out and looking for signs of growth.

Jesus' incarnational ministry took him to the places where people naturally met—lakesides, wells, market places, even synagogues and temples if he had to. At the heart of the *Pints of View* pub event is a desire to put ourselves in the places where ordinary people meet, not tucked away timidly, and to make ourselves visible and our apologetics unapologetic.

At heart we are communicating a self-giving God who entered into the rough and tumble of human life

The Twelve were sent to respond to what they found. In the same way, we have no prior knowledge of who exactly will be there, or the questions that they will raise. And yet we are confident that whatever does come up we will have something to say. Not because we are confident in our ability to address any given topic, but because at heart we are communicating a self-giving God who entered into the rough and tumble of human life, and who is intimately concerned with every facet of it. There are no off-limit topics for an incarnational God. Neither is anything which genuinely concerns or confuses one of his children too trivial or insignificant. If it really matters to them, it really matters.

Relational Mission—Jesus the Befriender

Jesus demonstrates a model of mission that encompasses both the deliberate and strategic, and the seemingly random, personal, intimate chance encounter. In fact, he invests time in a variety of encounters, some of which lead him into relationships that prove to be strategic for the rest of his ministry, while others are simply about responding to the needs of a particular individual at a particular time. The kingdom of God was demonstrated in the way Jesus responded to these individuals. The heart of Jesus' mission is restoring relationships.

The kingdom of God was demonstrated in the way Jesus responded to these individuals

His encounters with Zacchaeus (Luke 19.1–10) and the woman at the well (John 4.1–26) led to a transformation of themselves as well as the local community. The impression he made on some fishermen proved ultimately to transform relationships across the known world (Matthew 28.16–20). Jesus never saw a meeting as an irritation, he saw it as a catalyst for growth and change.

How open are we to the possibility that there are those outside the church who, like Zacchaeus and the woman at the well think that they are not worthy of our time and attention, but who will respond positively if we offer it?

Robust Debate and Mission

In Acts 17.19–34 we read about Paul debating at the Areopagus. This is not just a case of him going to where people gathered, but going to where they debated. Everybody there knew what to expect—Paul was welcomed because he understood the local culture and was able to speak into that culture with some wisdom and freshness. He played by the rules.

Pubs have long been places for discussion, debate and frank exchanges of views in our culture. If not quite an Areopagus, they contain more than a few amateur philosophers! They are an appropriate arena for debate. We are not inflicting our arguments on those who do not want to hear them, rather providing a forum for those who do want to listen, or have their thoughts and questions taken seriously.

Critical Engagement—Questioning and Answering

Taking people seriously and respecting their views is quite different from uncritical agreement. To take an idea seriously means to engage with it, to ask difficult questions of it. In doing so, new insights are gained, prejudices exposed, minds stretched. Robust debate is a commitment to serious engagement.

Rather than an adversarial model, where someone wins and someone loses, there is a commitment from everyone to ask questions of their own opinions. If we believe we have an answer worth hearing, the Word worth proclaiming, we should model a willingness to expose our understanding of it to difficult questions. Then we earn the right to have our critique of other contemporary philosophies heard.

Non-institutional Engagement
—The Missional Church at Work

The picture of the fledgling church that we see in Acts is of a church defined by an onward and outward movement, which results in growth. The early church has its identity most clearly expressed in mission.

In Britain, a church's identity is most often expressed institutionally. Buildings, liturgical practice and denominational structures shape a church's character and define the way it does things. It is easy to fall into the trap of rarely looking beyond those walls, and of failing to catch a glimpse of the Spirit's work elsewhere.

In Britain, a church's identity is most often expressed institutionally

When we seek to reach beyond the boundaries of the church, we exchange a safe and protected culture for a different one—one in which words, symbols and actions are interpreted differently. Not everyone in our churches may be comfortable with this cultural shift. Two illustrations from our experience show that this is a two-way process.

The first was a simple question that we had to address before we began our first evening. Should we drink as we normally would? Should we drink at all? Would some members of our church struggle with the idea of us, in our representative roles, promoting alcohol?

We would normally drink when in a pub with friends. We were aware that there were members of the church whose lives have been scarred by alcohol abuse, whether by themselves or others. And we knew that there would be those who simply would not like the idea. How different was the pub culture? What would it mean if we went into a pub event and then steadfastly stuck to soft drinks?

To go to a pub and not drink is to mark yourself out as different (or as a driver, but we both walked). We felt that to do so would give an impression of us being a bit aloof, not fully taking part or wanting to over-commit. This would create a barrier between ourselves and those we were meeting. At one level, of course, we are different. But that difference should not be defined by the things we do not do—rather by the positive things we embrace.

We felt that to engage incarnationally was to hold to our own integrity (we would usually drink socially) and to drink responsibly.

Christian institutions still managed to frustrate our attempts to engage with the people on the fringes of church, though, as the following story illustrates.

We felt that to engage incarnationally was to hold to our own integrity and to drink responsibly

In seeking to reach out in this way, it was important for us to connect with a culture in which beers and spirits are sold by clever, glossy advertising imagery. We hoped our publicity would get noticed and talked about, as well as demonstrate that we were taking the event seriously enough to invest in it. It conveyed a message that we value this opportunity to meet with you, and really want you to come.

Seeking to open the invitation to as many as possible, we approached schools who we already had a relationship with, to ask if they would distribute the publicity to parents. Our local state school was happy to do this. A nearby Church of England School refused to take the publicity. When we enquired why, we were informed that it might encourage children to drink alcohol (although of course this subtle message would never be communicated by them selling alcohol at events or running a bottle tombola at School Summer Fairs!). The local state school was pleased to help because they valued the relationship with the church and wanted to be supportive.

Making Connections—Everyday Faith, Everyday Life

Pints of View was begun as an attempt to connect everyday life with faith, so that faith is grounded and rooted in a way that makes a difference both to our understanding of life and how we choose to live it.

'Dave' was frustrated with conventional church. He felt that it was not addressing the questions he was asking or engaging with the issues he faced in his life and work. He came along because he thought that if our church could run this kind of event, then we might be able to help him relate his life and faith.

This connection between faith and the issues of everyday life also enhances its effectiveness as an evangelistic strategy. Rather than putting on evangelistic events that try to second-guess the issues that will connect with people, the questioner sets the agenda.

How many obstacles do we want to put in the way of those we are seeking to reach out to? So often the venue, the cultural assumptions, the language used, the length of the event, the expectation to join in and say things that might compromise someone's integrity, all conspire to act as barriers. *Pints of View* seeks not only to eliminate possible barriers, but actively find points of connection.

> *How many obstacles do we want to put in the way of those we are seeking to reach out to?*

In terms of evangelistic strategy, the enquirer is not forced into a 'church culture' event, and theology or Christian teaching is done implicitly rather than explicitly (in the main) and the terminology and language used is drawing primarily on non-church culture. In addition, the Christian faith is demonstrated to have something of value to say about the whole of life.

On one occasion we turned up half an hour before the event, and found that one of the tables right in the middle of our usual area was already taken, by a young man and two young women. In preparing the area, we began chatting with them, and explained what was about to happen, and asked if that was OK with them. They were fine, and said 'No, you carry on, we're going soon.'

The event started, and the people at the table were chatting away, and sometimes listening in to the event. Someone than asked a question about asylum seekers and illegal immigration, and particularly about new Government legislation placing the onus for ensuring that lorries were not carrying illegal immigrants on the drivers. We responded to the question, and said that we felt it was unfair to punish lorry drivers for another individual's illegal actions. At this point the young bloke at the table, turned round and joined in, telling us that he was a long-distance lorry driver who was just passing through. He engaged with the discussion with a lot of passion and then he and his friends continued to do so as we talked about other issues, and he raised genuine questions of faith. Afterwards we chatted

> *He was amazed the clergy were doing something like this, and felt able to talk openly about his life and beliefs*

some more with him. He was amazed the clergy were doing something like this, and felt able to talk openly about his life and beliefs. All this happened because we had chatted with them, and then found a point of contact which nobody would have predicted beforehand.

Conscientization—Opening Eyes, Challenging Preconceptions

One of the underlying principles of Liberation Theology is the process of conscientization. This process involves a commitment to uncovering the truth of a situation and to having our eyes opened to vested interests, hidden motives and the power-structures involved.

Conscientization is a process of questioning that which we tend to receive uncritically. If someone has read the same newspaper all their adult life, or always watches the same television programmes (or has always attended the same church…!) they will have been shaped by that process. The information they have received has been consciously edited—some facts selected, some arguments ignored—before it is transmitted to, and received by, them. We all have prejudices and beliefs; we do not always know who has shaped them, or their motives in doing so.

In Romans chapter 12 Saint Paul urges Christian believers

Do not conform any longer to the pattern of this world, but be transformed by the renewing of your mind. Then you will be able to test and approve what God's will is—his good, perfect and pleasing will.

At *Pints of View* we have attempted to help people to begin a process of conscientization, in order to filter and challenge the information they receive, and to ask questions of it from an informed, Christian viewpoint. In doing this we have helped them to 'be transformed by the renewing of their minds.'

4

<h1 style="text-align:right">DIY Pints of View</h1>

So you quite like the idea of an established pub Questions and Answers session?

A packed room hanging on your every word, an ever changing cast of local and regional guest speakers to inform, entertain and challenge, the buzz of thinking on your feet, never knowing what the next question will be. But how do you get there from here? Just follow a few straightforward steps...

Find a Venue

This is the first and most important step. The venue you choose will have the single biggest effect on the success of your pub event. Key questions to ask are:

Will we be welcome? You may instinctively think, 'Pubs won't want a bunch of Christians coming in.' But think again! Pubs are businesses, and operate on the bottom line. Many pubs, particularly some national chains, are seeking to broaden their appeal and bring in new customers. If there is an evening in the week when you know the pub is only a third full, and a large enough area could be made available to you, many pub managers will be more than happy to push their sales figures up.

Can we be heard? Some pubs operate a music free policy. If the pub you have in mind does not, it will be very hard to run a *Pints of View* event there. As the event grows, the use of sound reinforcement may be necessary to enable everybody to hear. Is the pub likely to allow this?

Is it a place people want to come to? Will members of my congregation and their friends find this a safe place to come to? Is it a place where they will feel able to be themselves? When scouting out possible pubs, go with one or two people you think might be interested in the event and take a look together, ask them how they feel there. Do you stand out? If you do when you are just having a quiet drink and a chat, and feel uncomfortable, you definitely will when you try and stand up and speak about a Christian perspective on abortion, asylum seekers or euthanasia.

Is it easily accessible? Who do you envisage coming? Where are they coming from? A pub in a shopping area in a central position may be better than a pub situated on a main road roundabout.

Is there an area within the pub which is suitable? The Bar Manager or Landlord will be unlikely to let you go anywhere which prevents people getting access to the bar to get served. Equally you may not want to be in the busiest area as that will be noisiest. Is there a self-contained, but still open, area, so that people can listen in, see you each month and gradually be drawn in? Separate function rooms have a marked 'threshold' to cross, and you and your churchy friends bolting into them may give an impression of a secret society, closed to non-members, rather than a confident, approachable, open group.

Build a Relationship with the Pub

In order for the event to work, the ongoing relationship with the pub is crucially important. If you only go in on the night of the event you may quickly be seen as a group who are 'using' the pub. If you make the pub your own local, pop in for meals, and are seen as a normal customer sometimes, it will help others to relate to you, and you will more quickly earn the trust of staff and regulars. Peter has arranged to meet people enquiring about baptisms, weddings and funerals in the pub in Boldmere, and on other occasions has bumped into contacts from pastoral ministry.

If you only go in on the night of the event you may quickly be seen as a group who are 'using' the pub

Never take your relationship with the pub for granted. After the first few events ask the duty manager if it was OK, and as you come to the end of your first year, and you wish to carry on, check that that will be alright, and confirm the personal conversation in writing, confirming the dates for the forthcoming year—preferably before you have expensive publicity produced!

The pub in Boldmere is part of the Wetherspoon's chain, and towards the end of the first year of doing *Pints of View* we were featured in their national magazine. This was a good piece of publicity for us, but also raised the profile of the pub in the company, which reflected well on the pub manager.

Branding and Publicity

When we began the event, we produced low-cost publicity, which was mostly to provide information about an event which was to happen in the very near future—it was expected to be read and thrown away. When we decided to re-launch the following year as an on-going event, we wanted to begin to build a brand.

The idea was to give out something which would make an immediate impact on those who came to church that Christmas, to be a bit 'In your face' and surprise them with the image, humour and the unexpected professionalism of the presentation. This showed that we valued the event enough to invest in it. The publicity was good enough for people to give to friends without embarrassment, and long-lasting enough to keep for the year as a reminder. By ordering thousands we were able to keep on bombarding people as well!

Each year we then came up with a new and different advertising campaign. The text on the back remained largely unchanged, emphasizing the content of the event in a very clear straightforward way, and naming the vicar, who is the embodiment of brand of the local church.

Even if people who came to the church at Christmas would not want to come to the event, the publicity they received reinforced key messages about the church and our faith: 'We're not scared;' 'Our faith is real world;' 'Christian faith has something to say about current affairs.' This backed up the themes of our preaching over Christmas, and showed that we wanted to put them into practice.

Pulling Together a Team

At the outset it is important to have a core group of people who are committed to the event for the duration—to be there each month, to ask questions when no-one else will, to bring along friends, and to help build the atmosphere, and model good listening! If someone new comes along and there are only three people there, they will feel vulnerable and that the event is not up to much. If you already have a crowd formed, there will be a buzz about the event, and newcomers can have safe anonymity, and enter into things at their own pace.

It is important to have a core group of people who are committed to the event for the duration

As the event grows and is established, team members can also help to prepare the room (it is not reasonable to expect the bar staff to move tables or chairs before or after the event), replenish the glasses of speakers(!), give out publicity, and be aware of people on the fringe.

Also challenge those in your church who will not come themselves to support the event with their prayers.

Preparation

So you are about to answer a series of questions on absolutely anything. How do you prepare? From experience we can say that nearly all the questions have been triggered by something that has been in the news in the preceding week. People do not attend these events to hear an expert lecture on them. They go to be stimulated and to think for themselves. Sometimes it is important to say 'I don't know' or 'I'm not sure.' Sometimes it is useful to pull out one or two key points from a particular subject area and seek to explain Christian principles which guide our response. It is important that speakers are allowed to disagree, as with many of these issues the honest response is to say there is not one Christian catch-all answer on this, but these are the important issues involved, which leads me to settle on this side of the argument.

The most helpful resource in preparing for *Pints of View* has been Radio Five Live. After 9 o'clock each morning it has had phone-in debate programmes. These help you to hear the issues which people are concerned about and to digest some of the arguments on each side. It is most important to watch or listen to the news on the day of the event, as most questions are thought up on the night.

In essence the task of the speaker is to reflect theologically, and to articulate the process of asking critical questions

In essence the task of the speaker is to reflect theologically, and to articulate the process of asking critical questions about the issues raised. In-depth knowledge is not therefore required—the ability to understand the issues well enough to raise our own intelligent questions is. But when out of your depth, stop splashing about! Just follow a few straightforward steps.

Keeping the Momentum Going

Over the five years at Boldmere, there have been periods where *Pints of View* has felt a little flatter, where things have started to get a little predictable, where the same tried questions kept being asked. (The complexity of an event like this is that they may have been real questions to the person asking them). To help keep the momentum we invited a number of guest speakers.

Sometimes these were guest speakers invited to answer general questions from a Christian perspective as usual. These have included a parliamentary candidate, a number of bishops, and other senior clergy.

More recently we searched for Christian guests with specific areas of expertise who could address questions in this area coherently for a whole themed

Guests on the panel add a new perspective and a different voice

evening of questions. for example, a High Court judge, an oncologist, and an Islamicist.

Guests on the panel add a new perspective and a different voice. If chosen carefully they can also draw in people who have not been to the event previously. They can often speak with authority, and challenge in ways that those of us who have to speak to the people again on Sunday may not be able to.

Step out in Faith

That is our DIY guide to *Pints of View*, but it is worth bearing in mind that each and every one of those lessons has been learnt by experience—the only real way to learn how to 'do it yourself' is to get on with 'doing it.'

The first stage for you might be to round up ten people from your church, and arrange to meet up with them one evening down the pub to chat and ask questions about the burning issues of the day, and how our faith should guide our thinking about them. That would help you, and them, to get used to doing theology on the hoof, and connecting our Christian faith with venues other than our homes or our churches.

The Art of Answering Questions 5

So we have convinced you to give it a go, you have found the perfect pub, which serves the perfect pint, and you have advertised your event to the right people and are sure they are going to turn up.

The days are ticking by, and the event is looming. How do you prepare for an event when you do not know which questions will come up?

Be Prepared

Having spoken on the panels for these events for a little while now we can say with a degree of confidence that the questions you will be asked fall into three main categories, and the way you prepare for each is slightly different:

1 Current Affairs

Think about it…your audience will be made up of some people who plan in advance, who will know they are coming to the event and give some thought to what questions they might ask. And then there are the other ones who will just ask whatever comes into their head. That is most likely to be whatever is current—what they saw on the News as they ate their tea that evening or what was on the radio as they drove home from work, or on the front page of the newspaper. In our experience these make up the majority of questions.

So how best to prepare for this sort of question? A commitment to keeping up to date with what is going on across the world in politics, trade and ethics is essential. While you do not have to know everything, you need to show yourself to be informed. This is not as hard as it might seem. Regular reading of the paper (or online news sites) and listening to the radio or television provides the background necessary for you to reflect on.

There is a further tip we can suggest. Try to tap in to the news sources which your audience will be influenced by, as what will be the hot topic in one newspaper may not be the lead story in another. Particularly helpful are radio phone-ins,

While you do not have to know everything, you need to show yourself to be informed

as they give a sense of which issues in a particular debate really matter to people, and of the national mood. Many different points are made in a short space of time, and the panellists are forced to think on their feet.

2 Old Chestnuts

Many of the questions we have been asked fall into one of eight broad categories:

- **Medical Ethics**—euthanasia, cloning, abortion, use of resources within the Health Service
- **Law and Order**—justice and punishment, gun control, drug policy
- **Sexuality and sexual morality**—attitudes to sexual orientation, politicians'/celebrities' private lives, changing values
- **Business and Financial Ethics**—investments, workplace attitudes
- **Development and World Trade**—fair trade, debt cancellation
- **Media Influence**—how news is reported, censorship, relationship of the media to other institutions (Hutton Report)
- **Global Political crises**—Iraq war, Zimbabwe, Northern Ireland, Israel and Palestine
- **Religious**—creation, 'Where is God in...?,' How does God answer prayer?
- **Nationalism and racial identity**—immigration policy, racism, responses to people of other faiths, 'British' identity.

You may be reasonably confident in your ability to answer questions on some, or even all, of these topics. If you are aware of areas where you would not be strong then there are apologetics books on these subjects which address frequently asked questions. The magazine *Third Way* provides informed and challenging Christian comment on a breadth of cultural, social and political issues. Grove Ethics Series may not provide the last word on some of these subjects '...but often the first.' If you are aware that a particular subject holds particular interest for your audience then consider inviting guest speakers to address those areas.

The final thing to remember when a question is asked which we may feel we have done to death in previous months is that what might be an old chestnut to us might be a real concern to the person asking the question.

3 Local Debates

When local issues are raised, it pays you to tread very carefully—what you say may have pastoral ramifications. Whilst a throw away comment in a pub in the West Midlands on a wet Monday in February is unlikely to be reported back to the Prime Minister, if it is about the Headteacher of the local school or the Councillor they may get to hear about it. Also, people have interested opinions on matters of great importance, such as debt relief or nuclear power, and are able to debate and disagree on such things as adults. But when it comes to saying whether a local park should be built on, objectivity can fly out of the window.

4 The Wildcard

This is the Joker in the pack, the left-field, blue sky thinking, out-of-the-box and off-the-planet question. These come up rarely, and are usually either due to a) a particular minority fascination of the individual in question b) a deliberate attempt to catch out the panellists or c) a particularly strong guest beer! If it is a) spend as little time as possible on it, or invite comments from others as soon as possible to see if anyone else is interested. If it is b) and they have stumped you, a little bit of humility is a good thing, and if you handle it with good humour you will probably enhance your standing with the group. If it is c) have a couple of pints yourself, and soon everything will become clearer.

Theological Reflection

We run this event to help people to think Christianly about real life. The individual issues raised, and answers given to them, are of secondary importance compared to the process of inviting people to reflect with us as we ask the important questions, and bring the insights of the Christian tradition to bear upon them.

We run this event to help people to think Christianly about real life

By reflecting on current events, and asking where God is in them, we are helping people to begin to undertake this process for themselves. This is partly about challenging the assumptions that many hold, and critiquing them, and also about challenging the means by which we receive the news and other information we base our decisions on.

For those who do not yet have a Christian commitment, we show that Christian faith has something to say about, and a challenge to bring to, every area of life. For those who are already committed Christians, the process of reflecting on the issues of everyday life is a crucial part of mature Christian discipleship.

Comments from the Floor

There will be times when the most informed person on a particular subject is not one of the panellists. The important thing as a panellist is to then bring reflection and critical engagement to what they are saying. I do not know as much about genetics as a consultant doctor, but I can ask them challenging questions from a Christian perspective.

From a practical viewpoint inviting comments from the floor gives panellists time to think, or gives everyone a rest from hearing the same voice. Particularly in the early stages, inviting people to comment helps them to feel part of the event. It offers people their moment in the spotlight, and some people seem to relish that. The only thing to watch is that you do not allow them to over-dominate, as others in the audience may resent that.

Acknowledging Doubt and Uncertainty

There is a strength in being honest and saying 'I don't know.' It affirms the fact that everybody has doubts and insecurities. And it undermines the wrong preconception, that many have, that you need a completely certain belief in every area in order to be a Christian. It acknowledges our partial access to knowledge—we do not have all the information, let alone all the answers.

If we always answer categorically then we do not allow ourselves any room for manoeuvre

We can model engaging and wrestling with issues, often by voicing the questions which we ourselves are asking. We might have different perspectives and points to make a couple of years down the line. If we always answer categorically (and our audience have long memories) then we do not allow ourselves any room for manoeuvre.

Encouraging Debate

A pub is a place of debate. It is the Areopagus of contemporary society. It is a place where conversation is not private, but public, and where we can be overheard and our comments spark contributions that we may not have invited.

Some people are highly opinionated and used to speaking in public, others more reserved or shy. Whilst we cannot be held accountable for comments expressed by others, or the way that they express them, one of the roles of the panel is to model attitudes which encourage all to contribute. A golden rule to remember is that we need to show respect to others' viewpoints in order to gain respect for our own.

Holding on to Your Integrity

In the heat of the moment, there is always a temptation to please the crowd. It is easier to agree with people than to disagree with them. But what if we genuinely disagree? Affirming people without agreeing with them is a difficult balancing act. It is right to dare to speak against the mood of the crowd, and to have the confidence to make a point and let it stand without having to force people to agree with it.

Stand-up comedians sometimes deal with hecklers by making them look foolish. No matter how tempting, we should not give in to that temptation. The point is that if people who disagree with us are put down, the unspoken message is that only clergy are right, that the powerful have a voice and as a consequence people will no longer wish to volunteer their thoughts. Sometimes it is worth losing the argument to win the person.

Having Fun

This is an enjoyable event. It is unpredictable, with an element of risk. Use humour to relax the atmosphere. Once people get to know each other, and feel safe, the dynamic allows for banter that communicates a genuine warmth.

6   Where Do You Go From Here?

The short answer is 'down the pub.'

The slightly longer answer is to talk to a group from your church and begin to think through the possibilities in your area. Visit a few different pubs and find out which ones might be most likely to receive you warmly, which you feel most comfortable in, which you can hear yourself think in.

For more information, to ask questions, to build up a network of churches running *Pints of View* events, to swap ideas and suggestions for guest speakers, and to find out how to access the full colour publicity designs, visit our website www.pintsofview.org.uk

Talk to a group from your church and begin to think through the possibilities in your area

Remember, *Pints of View* is not a blueprint but rather a framework that needs rooting in your situation. Your new *Pints of View* event will reveal new ways of doing things, which draw on your gifts, and work in your setting.

Will this be yet another book that will be sat back on your shelf to enjoy a lengthy and peaceful retirement? Or will it lead to good social nights out with a growing group of friends, for whom faith is increasingly important?

The choice is yours.